GHOST STORIES

GHOSTS IN HOTELS

By Lisa Owings

BELLWETHER MEDIA • MINNEAPOLIS, MN

EPIC BOOKS are no ordinary books. They burst with intense action, high-speed heroics, and shadows of the unknown. Are you ready for an Epic adventure?

This edition first published in 2017 by Bellwether Media, Inc.

No part of this publication may be reproduced in whole or in part without written permission of the publisher.
For information regarding permission, write to Bellwether Media, Inc., Attention: Permissions Department,
5357 Penn Avenue South, Minneapolis, MN 55419.

Library of Congress Cataloging-in-Publication Data

Names: Owings, Lisa, author.
Title: Ghosts in Hotels / by Lisa Owings.
Description: Minneapolis, MN : Bellwether Media, Inc., [2017] | Series: Epic.
   Ghost Stories | Audience: Ages 7-12. | Audience: Grades 2 to 7. |
   Includes bibliographical references and index.
Identifiers: LCCN 2016002570 | ISBN 9781626174283 (hardcover : alk. paper)
Subjects: LCSH: Haunted hotels–Juvenile literature. | Ghosts–Juvenile
   literature.
Classification: LCC BF1474.5 .O95 2017 | DDC 133.1/22–dc23
LC record available at http://lccn.loc.gov/2016002570

Printed in the United States of America, North Mankato, MN.

TABLE OF CONTENTS

HAUNTED HOTELS

It is late at night. You check into your hotel room and climb into bed. In the morning, your suitcase has moved. But no one else is with you.

Many people pass through hotel doors. How many never check out?

SOUNDS IN THE NIGHT

Colorado's Stanley Hotel seems full of ghostly guests. Many visitors go there hoping to be spooked.

One of the hotel's most haunted rooms is 418.

Stanley Hotel, Colorado

N
W · E
S

HISTORY CONNECTION

F.O. Stanley opened the Stanley Hotel in 1909. He came to Colorado to improve his health. The fresh mountain air was good for him.

BEHIND THE SHINING

Horror author Stephen King stayed at the Stanley Hotel. The trip gave him the idea for *The Shining*.

Guests in 418 often hear children playing in the hall. One couple said noisy children had kept them up all night.

The couple complained to staff the next morning. But the staff said no children had stayed there that night.

A FRIENDLY GHOST

The ghost of a boy haunts 418. He wakes children to play at night. He tickles them or shakes their beds.

Visitors in 418 also notice something strange about the beds. They sometimes have body-shaped **impressions**.

Could ghost children be napping after playing all night?

SIGHTINGS AT THE STANLEY HOTEL

- **Mr. Stanley standing in the billiard room and lobby**
- **Mrs. Stanley playing piano in the ballroom**
- **Lord Dunraven stealing jewelry from fourth floor rooms**
- **Maid Elizabeth cleaning the room where she was hurt in an explosion**
- **Children playing or calling for their nanny**

TOUCHED BY EVIL

RMS *Queen Mary*,
California

The RMS *Queen Mary* was once a working ship. Now it is a hotel docked off the California coast.

HISTORY CONNECTION

The *Queen Mary* first sailed in 1936. It carried the wealthy across the Atlantic Ocean. During World War II, it brought soldiers to battle. The ship stopped sailing in 1967.

Many people died aboard the *Queen Mary*. Do they now haunt the hotel?

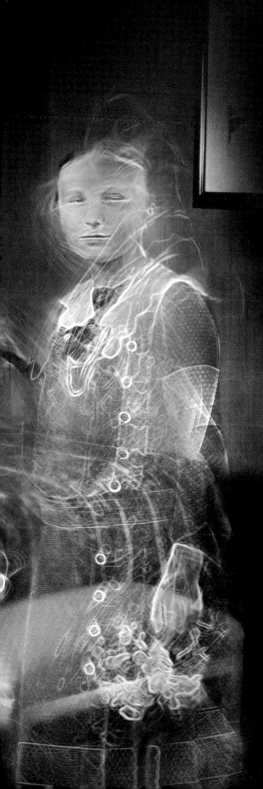

One ghost story tells of a **tragedy** in 1959. A family was killed in room B474. Their spirits may **linger** at the scene of their death. Guests have recorded voices in the empty room. Some report being touched by ghostly hands!

IS IT REAL?

Similar stories are told about room B340. A ghost hunting team explored it. They filmed a bed sheet moving on its own. But many believe the video was faked.

One man stayed in the room next to B474. He felt something evil coming from the closet. The whole room seemed to fill with anger. Then a male ghost appeared. Could this ghost have been the killer?

SIGHTINGS ON THE RMS QUEEN MARY

- Screams near the bow of the ship
- A worker in overalls near the engine room
- Wet footprints around the dry, empty pool
- A woman in a white gown in the lounge

17

REAL GHOSTS OR SPOOKED GUESTS?

Ghost stories draw many guests to haunted hotels. They want to believe that the stories are true.

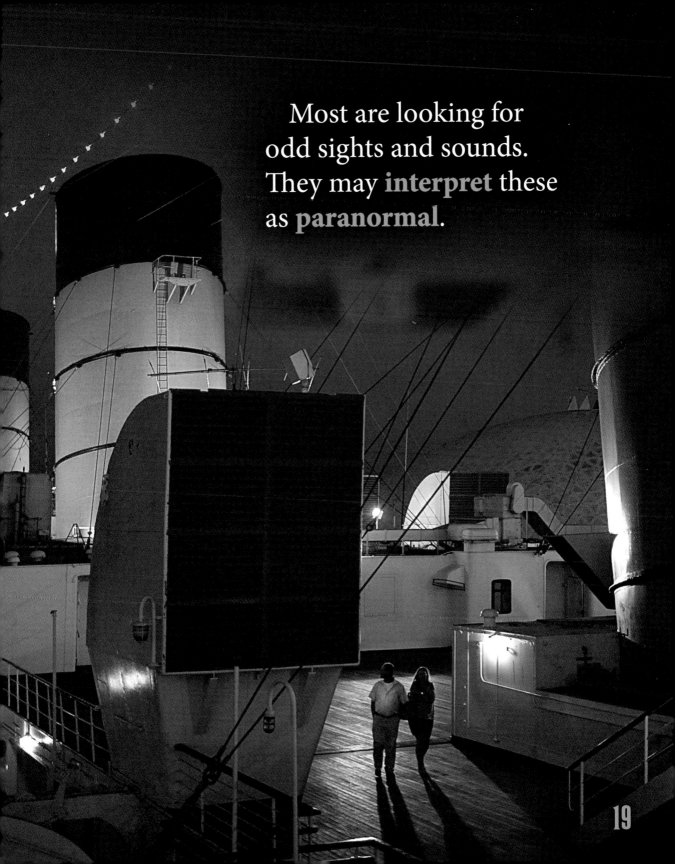

Most are looking for odd sights and sounds. They may **interpret** these as **paranormal**.

Many people see or hear strange things while falling asleep. **Sleep paralysis** can cause people to see ghostly figures. Do hotel guests experience this more often? Perhaps. Or maybe you will meet a real ghost on your next getaway!

SLEEP TIGHT

Sleep paralysis can happen when you wake from deep sleep. Your body cannot move. But your mind might still be dreaming.

GLOSSARY

impressions—marks made by pressing into something

interpret—to understand something based on personal beliefs

linger—to remain

paranormal—strange and not able to be explained by science

sleep paralysis—a state between sleep and waking in which a person is briefly unable to move or speak

tragedy—a very sad event that often involves a death

TO LEARN MORE

AT THE LIBRARY

Higgins, Nadia. *Ghosts*. Minneapolis, Minn.: Bellwether Media, 2014.

Keene, Carolyn. *The Mystery at Lilac Inn*. Bedford, Mass.: Applewood Books, 1994.

Von Finn, Denny. *Stanley Hotel*. Minneapolis, Minn.: Bellwether Media, 2014.

ON THE WEB

Learning more about ghosts in hotels is as easy as 1, 2, 3.

1. Go to www.factsurfer.com.

2. Enter "ghosts in hotels" into the search box.

3. Click the "Surf" button and you will see a list of related web sites.

With factsurfer.com, finding more information is just a click away.

INDEX

The images in this book are reproduced through the courtesy of: Ysbrand Cosijn, front cover (ghost); Peter Talke Photography, front cover (background), pp. 1, 8-9 (background); aboikis, pp. 4-5 (ghost); dvoevnore, pp. 4-5 (suitcase); Petar Djordjevic, pp. 4-5 (background); Robert Kelsey, p. 7; CHRISTOPHE ROLLAND, pp. 8-9 (ghosts); Thaweewong Vichaiururoj, p. 10 (ghost); fivepointsix, p. 10 (background); holbox, p. 13; Galyamin Sergej, pp. 14-15 (ghost father, ghost daughter middle-top, ghost mother); Roman Nerud, pp. 14-15 (ghost daughter right, ghost daughter bottom-middle); Neil Setchfield/ Alamy, pp. 14-15 (background); Stokkete, pp. 16-17 (ghost); Paul Briden/ Alamy, pp. 16-17; Helen H. Richardson/ Getty Images, p. 18; John Schreiber/ ZUMA Press, p. 19; Sergey Mironov, pp. 20-21 (woman); MadeByEve, pp. 20-21 (ghost); Sergey Chirkov, pp. 20-21 (background).